I0490092

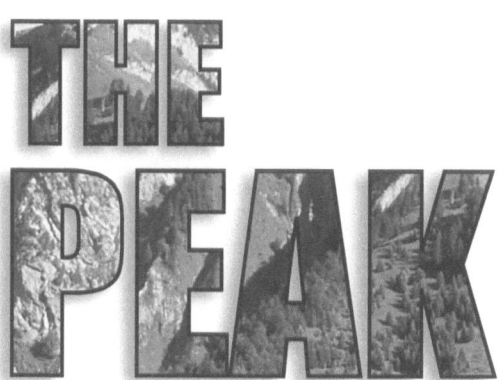

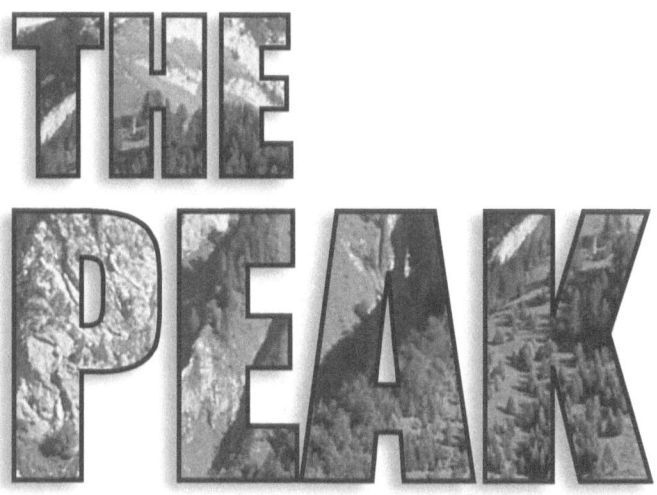

THE PEAK

AISHA NAIM

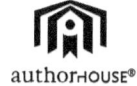

authorHOUSE®

AuthorHouse™ UK Ltd.
1663 Liberty Drive
Bloomington, IN 47403 USA
www.authorhouse.co.uk
Phone: 0800.197.4150

Published by AuthorHouse 11/12/2013

ISBN: 978-1-4918-7760-9 (sc)
ISBN: 978-1-4918-7761-6 (e)

Let's praise the Lord great,
Who made showers, flowers, and fragrance;
Ordained people to love, not hate
Filled our hearts with emotion and grace.

I dedicate this book to my parents, Naim-ul-Imam and Kaneez-e-Fatima. I could not have written it without their love, support, and encouragement.

Contents

1   What Failure Says about Your Success 1

2   Money Is Not Honey 2

3   The Peak 4

4   New Era 8

5   The Bird 10

6   North Park 12

7   Herald 14

8   Glow-Worms 16

9   Devotion 19

10   Murmur of the River 20

11   Unkempt Gardens 23

12   Time 26

13   Away from This World 28

14   Journey 30

15   Dragon of the Lake 32

16   Eastern Woman 35

17   Statue 37

18   The Sea 39

19   A Wander in the Woods 42

20   Under the Sunshine 44

21   For 5 July 46

22   It's Me 47

23   Deep Shadows 48

24   Fear 50

25   Flood of Rain 52

What Failure Says about Your Success

Effort is never put forth in vain.
Keep going; you aren't late.
You must something gain.
You yourself will determine your fate.

Don't let failures make you miserable.
Keep trying, and remember:
Only shaped diamonds are valuable.
You, too, one day will be greater.

A great man reaches any height
By means of his patience.
Nobody achieves sudden flight.
You, though, will fly, given your perseverance.

You will learn by your mistakes
And discover the right rule to win.
"Don't put on the brakes,"
Your failure says with a grin.

Money Is Not Honey

The people who love money
Think that it is honey.
They hope more friends to make
And that their joyful lives will never end.
Death shouts, "You must be awake
Always; you can't have money as your friend."

Your money attracts flatterers, who surround you.
You may enjoy their company when you are blue.
But soon, they will leave you without wit
And much farther from the truth.
One day, nobody will care for you a bit.
You may waste your power and youth.

Great kings who had money and treasure
Weren't able to buy pleasure.
Their money and popularity died with their death.
Nobody may have everlasting money.
Nothing can save one's life except one's own worth.
Those kings would be alive if they had had any.

Only worth and ability make a person live forever.
Those who understand this will always be alive, like
Shakespeare.
Prove your worth and your ability,
You may enjoy your days of joy.
But don't waste your life in futility.
Follow my advice and be sincere guy.

The Peak

I am going to touch the peak. I'm going to reach the top
Of this massive, mammoth mountain. I won't give up.
My dreams and ambitions are my rungs;
My brain, body, and energy are my tools.
With this act, I hope to become differentiated.
From those around me, I'll be separated.
I hope to find fragrance, peace, life, and serenity,
Splendour, magnificence, beauty, and eternity.

The tempest says,

"Ha ha ha, I'm full of violent puffs.
Your edifice built on trust will be shaken by my gusts.
Your being'll be torn apart by my wild whiffs.
I'll throw you right down those steep-sided cliffs."

The climber replies,

"I can do it; I will win.
I will get by; I won't pack it in.
My firm determination will act as a stirrup.
That shining destination is luring me up.
My leading resolution will suffice
To weaken your powerful puffs and whiffs.
The Lord's love will pull me through;
In His name, and with His support, I could get through."

After a month of toil, the climber says,

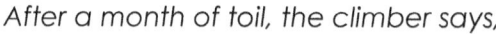

"Thirty days now on this cold and brutal precipice.
Piercing, freezing storm, born of ice,
Seems never to stop. My blood is freezing
My limbs, my face. This place is so haunting.
I need some warmth in order to move on,
Or at least a few tender words, which would sound sweet like a
song.
I am so alone in my agony and gloom.
The buds of my dream may never yet bloom."

"Life is always like this.
We never acquire the desired bliss
I will trample my wishes on my way down
To the ground, where hopes are all strewn.
This cold pain leaves my body curled up, and shuddered.
I know not how to rekindle the warmth inside.
The real battle is with myself, with my being—
My hunger, my rest, my emotion, and my longing."

The image of Father appears and speaks:

"My dear son, how can you let these petty storms
Bring you down? This may be done only by demise.
Son, in you I have full faith.
A man should struggle till his last breath,
You can fight all storms, but eternity.

For you, the powerful, nothing is a calamity.
These hurdles are meant to filter out your essence,
To reinforce your compliance and defiance.

The tempest speaks again:

"Not a single man can reach the peak.
It's very high, blighted, and bleak.
No man should see this dream, this wish,
As doable. I am here to make hopes dash."

Father's image speaks again:

"My son, the whole world stands for you.
Your virtue and toil make it bow down before you.
Fruit-bearing trees, flowers, roaring rivers,
And panicked oceans exist to whittle away the woes,
By giving you jewels, fruits, and fragrance
To support your courage and magnificence.
Now you may move on without regret,
As you are cheered on. Stick to your original thought."

The climber replies,

"Now I vanquish my captivating despair,
My long-treasured fear, that impairing veneer.
Now my veins are lifted and warm.

Blood starts gushing with all drops in frame
As if those drops were ready to burst out
Long before, and to put every storm to rout.
My rest was but a breather on a breathtaking
Journey. Now, again making me clasping.

"My father's words pushed me to know
Myself, and my blood, which can blow
Apart anything that comes in. So, now I know
That I do have power to reach the mountain's brow.
Now I know that I can rip into the rolling fog,
Change the course of a gale with my shrug.
I'll pierce the bosom of this mammoth mountain.
God has given us power, which we shouldn't disdain".

"Now from the peak I can see the shining sun
Covering all the hills and valleys below in its shine.
The scent of success is emitting by the flowers
Around me: fresh green leaves and the prettiest roses.
Let me breathe here fully, once, and for the last time.
My triumph is short, but it is splendid and prime.
So weak and wan am I with hunger, cold, and pain.
Now I know that I'll never see this sun again."

New Era

This world is an arena of mistakes,
Fouls, and wrongs, and it is full of freaks.
No perfection is to be found here.
Fully ripened fruits leave the tree bare.

No sigh is long, no hand is hard.
Not for long a song can be heard
Why do the prettiest flowers fade so soon?
Why so short-lived is the light of moon?

An experienced mother cannot raise her kid.
New flowers come ahead to place a bid.
I welcome all new scents and buds,
But I have learned to respect the old ones.

Why is perfection destined to die?
And then the clumsy come to try.
This place is full of trial and test
We keep trying until we achieve our useless best.

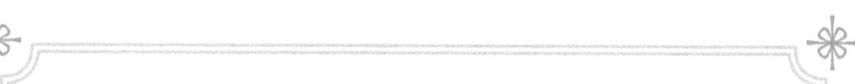

Lovely is the time you do have,

When you eat, love, and crave.

Feel full pleasure in all these moments combined.

So short is life designed.

Only if you set your heart on fire,

Very far may come your time to retire.

The Lord determines your lifespan so that you know the ways,

And He strings you along until you, finally float into the bays.

The Bird

Here I am surrounded by iron rods and despair.
A confining, crushing, small space with naught but food.
I can only feed myself like a gaffer.
I want to fly away and meet my brood.
I'm longing hard to rest my soul,
My heart, in a place where I may freely troll.

Just now—hurray!—by some chance, I see that the door was left
Open, mysteriously, or maybe by mistake.
Wow, I can see clear past the otherwise sight-hindering lot.
My heart urges me to fly away and break
The haunting well. I am for wide skies and open valleys,
For perching near the knolls, for flying high, and not for cages.

O you roaming, crooked cloud,
You envy my gaily zooming flight.
I just came out from beneath a dark shroud.
You will know what I mean if you roam in the light
After being in darkness. For this special happiness
Dream and desire to make it priceless.

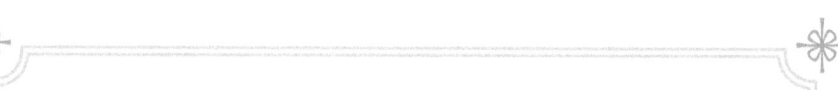

My wings are wide open. I am flying high, so high.
My bliss knows no bounds. My eyes are affixing
On marvellous sights. My heart does not sigh.
My flight is pepped; among the knolls I'm fleeting.
Just like this, every living being has a right to stay.
Why do the cruel confine and make us their prey?

North Park

This place never looked so beautiful before.
This fountain, situated at the park's core,
Seems to have a soul, which is going to utter
Words of blessing. Slender tubes of water
Sprinkle thousands of drops of water as if a mermaid
Were dispersing thousands of shining pearls from her hand.

The park is dotted with flowers of every colour,
And those colours are more radiant than ever.
Their movement is so lively; the flowers together look like
Small fairies dancing in unison, moving alike.
I never before saw such smiling roses or smelled such an
enchanting fragrance
As that which permeates this entire place.

A cool, refreshing breeze is reaching us sieving through the
leaves,
Making them rustle, which is enough to please
Our moods and refresh our minds. As their
Rustling movement makes a light music for
Our souls and minds. We both are lost
In this park, which is full of leaves' balmy scent.

Several times this place I visited.

Only today has it this special feeling incited.

Green-coloured grass, multicoloured flowers,

Pervasive balmy scents, and the music of leaves

Are performing their magic on me, and I sense

That all this is happening because of your lovely presence.

Herald

O you pink, pretty goddess,
You are mind-blowingly gorgeous.
You stand as a heron.
You shine in sun like pink silk.
Your flowers seem artistically woven
On boughs whereupon green leaves blend in with bark.

I am lost in my vision when a whiff of air
Makes you sprinkle pink petals onto the air.
Wow, that lofty sight took me
Into a fairyland where I beheld splendid scenes.
You waved as any pink fairy waves in glee,
Her magic wand releasing an abundance of shiny, pink stars.

You go as hundreds of light-emitting
Moths decide to go out: in one gathering.
You, goddess of nature, shower your shining
Pink petals to welcome every being
And make the earth velvety all summer long.
Your reply is instantaneous after every puff's calling.

I just want to sit down beneath you for a brief
When you bless me with showers of
Pleasant pink petals. I'd love to live those moments
Of life. Then I'd be lost. And I would love to say
In verse something that preserves these moments—
As a tribute to you, which I want to pay.

Glow-Worms

Paying her a visit was every other day's
Game. Going there was a great fun.
Gladdening childhood memories:
How we would play, jump, and run.
Mere trivialities were enough to provide us with fun.
How to her home we would always turn.

She was a goggle-eyed but a good-natured friend.
We loved her since she was a baker's daughter.
She'd give us fragrant, dyed
Cake crumbs, all different flavours together.
She'd serve those crumbs without a slight frown,
And we would impatiently gobble them down.

Once, in the gloaming near her home,
Our eyes glinted with great wonder
When hundreds of glow-worms created a glim,
Glittering and gliding here and there,
As if the alley had been filled with stars from the sky
And these shone all around us as they passed on by.

We rushed to catch the glow-worms while we poured
All the cake crumbs out of our pockets. Amid
That small rain of grain, we ran after to hold
Them. How many had we caught? Very few we held.
Our mad run behind them, our laughter, the time when we
were puerile—
Remembering our carefree life then often makes me smile.

*　　*　　*

Sometimes life shows us a reflection
Of an upcoming time through which we are to go.
The struggle, the affliction,
An array of troubles as we grow.
Very few opportunities we could hold, and for what price?
We realise only those that come to us by way of luck or
chance.

Happy moments come like glow-worms.
They light your life for a time.
You feel amazed and consider your poise;
You feel very far away from gloom.
You enjoy it when those glow-worms fly and emit their light,
But nothing can forever make life bright.

Very short is human life,

And shortest of all are the happy moments.

Rapturous time spans are so brief.

The beaming cluster of glow-worms is so spurious.

As very quickly away they fly.

If you hold them in your palm, they die.

Happy moments and glow-worms swiftly fly,

Making the alleyway of life dark again.

You miss them, and so you sigh.

You're left in the dark, groping your way again.

You look for them, you run behind.

They never come back; you may seek, but you may never find.

Devotion

A life dedicated to loved ones,
The planning, emotion, and intention.
All the dreams in your eyes
Find their way in one direction.

I saw it as uncommon when
We had struck up a conversation, laughed, and chatted,
And soon he showed love and devotion
For his family from deep within his heart.

He is the most kind-hearted and confident speaker
I have ever met. He knows how to mend his ways.
His pace, he knows how to measure.
His life, he chose to braze.

As the world is full of selfish desires
And mundane hearts, I admire
His love for his parents and sisters.
I wish him a triumphant emergence from every mire.

Murmur of the River

Near the river, sitting on a big boulder,
Deeply immersed in my thoughts,
I start but am unable to finish.
This is a beautiful riverbank,
And my mind is going blank.
I may yet find the end I wish.

What is the reason for my entity,
The meaning of my failure and success?
What is this world about?
I succeed, but it results in nothing.
I fail, but that, too, ends in nothing.
I can only feel and think about.

Gigantic thorny bushes surround me.
The more I untangle, the more they entangle me.
Through them I seek to make my path,
Trying hard to unknit and unknot.
If somehow I manage to get out,
Still, all courses of travel finally join up on the same path.

All movements are so empty and so shallow.
The world is like the tides of the deep sea.
They reach the shore with great enthusiasm
And energy, but to produce what fruit? They flow back
With nothing. Fervour is something they never lack.
They repeat their cresting and breaking, but this never seems
grim.

*   *   *

Continuously flowing river nearby me murmurs:
The time I move before falling into the sea is my time.
No matter that I am small, I make perfect waves.
My currents make music and happily dance.
I pave the way for coming currents, so as to give them chance.
It will be my triumph if they flow with ease.

Now I feel that I'm coming around to that way
Of thinking. Before falling into the sea,
I can make a pathway for others, and that is why
I tend towards growing the flowers of good deed
Lovely flowers that will keep this area scented
And fragrant for everyone who passes by.

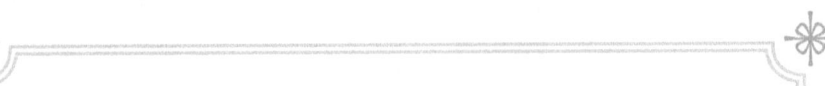

I began my walk to find some clue.
It was a very tiresome and long walk; I
Found nothing but empty valleys, barren roads, and
Deserted houses. I stopped at a place where
The soil was so soft, I dug it deeper
Sowed the seeds of drupes to reap some fruits from the ground.

Lovely flowers and fruit-laden trees will
Spread the message of love and humanity
For everyone who passes by. Your
Lord will choose a unicorn, beautiful and white,
To take you up into the valley, which is very bright,
And untangle all the knots to make your way clear.

Unkempt Gardens

I witnessed a teacher
Who frowned at the little boy's
Drawing when he had shown her
His incomplete landscape patches.

This attitude is never suitable for
A teacher. Her behaviour, which is
On display, is enough for
Disappointing young hearts and minds.

At this stage, when they are
In the process of making
Themselves, children need to see happier
Faces, which could help them smiling.

A seed properly grows into a plant
When it is surrounded by
Soft soil and receives a gardener's grant
Of love and care, which never lets it dry.

Young kids are like these seeds.
They need affection, compassion,
And care to grow into perfect human beings.
Only love and care can lead them to this destination.

I remember from my sweet school days
How I was scolded by a teacher one day
For forgetting some lessons.
I was scared and shaky the whole day.

The teacher's demeanour spoiled my abilities and my mood.
What good can come from a shaky body and a frightened
heart?
What new things can be brought about by a suppressed mind?
Fretting and discouraged, many children are left.

Suppressed souls do not dare rise.
Trampled hearts do not try to beam.
Controlled brains are unable to cause
Any good change; rather, they flow with the stream.

A gardener must be able to
Water and look after the flowers,
Giving buds the time they need to
Bloom and blend in with their surroundings.

A natural phenomenon: nature
Knows to head down the right path naturally.
If deviated from, the result may be disaster.
Hindering growth and life is an act done criminally.

Do not rush the budding sprouts.
Let the flowers blossom and scent
The garden in their own ways.
Let the world be fragrant.

Time

Now I am a mother of adult kids.
How lovely it is to see them
Grow, when their laughter fills all corners.
"Roses of my garden," I call them.

In the days when I taught them to walk,
To talk, to behave, to greet, and so on.
I performed all my duties and did all my work
In a spirit of trying to attain perfection.

Time has changed immensely, though; now
My children instruct me as if I am
A crawling child who needs to know
A whole lot about the world and groom.

Are new advancements and technology
Making the older generations ignorant? Are we left behind?
No, not really. This time is so creepy,
Fast, and dazzling that it makes some people blind.

I passed some of my days so perfectly and was so lively,
Fully bright, and up to date.
At their age, I was a prime girl of society.
Why are older ways now considered out of date?

Any day when the sun shines is the pinnacle,
Not the coming ones. That day is prime.
Just equip yourself to endure the present gale.
Then it is enough to be perfect in your own time.

Away from This World

The pain is so deep, and it breaks
My soul. How brutal is the world around me!
People's grisly attitudes and their darkness penetrates
My heart. How brutal is the world around me.
Even my dear relations have been polluted by materialism.
Our previous fellowship and sense of belonging is now covered
in grime.

I wish that, far, far away, I could fly
To a place where entities could let go and get by.

Let me take a breath and smile.
Let me live my life and enjoy
How freakish and meaningless they become in a while.
Let me heal from my sorrows. Do not make me cry.
I wish I could break all that comes across
My way so as to recover my happiness.

Very tired and broken, the world has gone colourless.
Will ever I find the right way
To live with that? Never, I guess.
Always with my tears I am forced to pay.
I wish I could mend my wounds and rest
In peace, which is something I never get.

They love me only when they are in need.
That is why no longer trusted are human beings.
The Lord asks us to give, not to hold,
Our affection, care, and loving feelings.
Towards the heights of pride and status they fly,
But people are meant to live on earth, not in the sky.

I wish that far, far away I could fly
To a place where entities could let go and get by.

They gave me the great gift of isolation
Much better than being with them.
It places my mind in an elevated position.
I am purged by my grief and gloom.
Here I can build my own castles, my own pleasure land,
Where pride, vanity, and competition do not descend.

Journey

Very dark, calm, and spiralling, here I'm standing
On stairs, without knowing how to turn the light on.
Willing to go up, my heart is throbbing.
It's so dark here, but with light I can move on.
Hesitant, reluctant, but very impatient,
I may move ahead if I find something bright.

Yes, I stepped up. Oh, I see some mirrors, but blurred.
A gallery of unclear images and confusing circles,
Dark, disgusting squares; this place is too old,
Filled with the images of pretty dancers
Drooping flowers around brave knights.
I also see deserted babies and filthy shapes.

Still confused, I find someone's hand.
It is very soft, compassionate, and full of warmth.
Radiant and glimmering existence endowed
Me with light to reveal my worth,
Making everything glisten around me.
Now the place is comprehensible to me.

The confusing circles are colourful rainbows.
I see clearly my image in that mirror.
What am I, as it shows?
Thick dust and dirt, visions unclear.
They can be bright and clear, and them we can mend
If we are given, as we all have the need for, a hand.

Dragon of the Lake

I remember we all used to play
Here, a place so green and charming.
We fondly made pots of clay.
Our careless running and wild capering!

How we would rest near this awesome
Lake, surrounded by huge oaks.
Larks would perch on branches and fill the evening time
With their sweet, musical chirrups.

One day the lake water started
Whirling in circles, and for a few days
The transparent, clear water of the lake converted
Into dark grey, with a few black patches.

And then suddenly we beheld a huge volution
From within the water, which lifted up and up
And turned into a gigantic, horrific dragon.
It was a damned creature, evidently corrupt.

Its ghastly appearance and loathsome expression
Appeared from the lake. Its big feet's thuds echoed
Widely across our beloved town.
The dragon bellowed; his eyes darted around.

Soon it was the main city he paced towards.
Once there, he started eating up human beings' hearts.
With his big claws,
Which he'd pierce and press into their chests.

Chaos and anarchy overran the city.
Thousands succumbed to the creature's endless hunger.
A wave of fear engulfed the place completely.
People ran, their faces pale and full of fear.

Now nobody cares for others, but only for their own lives.
They have no emotion and no feeling, and lost is the ancient
creed.
Badly trampled are the flowers and leaves.
Ties are loose; what a mad stampede.

Millions of heartless, stinking, dead bodies
Litter the ground. Now few are left with hearts.
Hopelessly, they are hiding in the corners,
Trying to save their lives and hearts.

On a very high mound in the north,
Breezes are magical, truly marvellous.
Expensive but hollow outfits are moving on the path
Leading to a huge, shiny house.

I saw only clothes, with no bodies inside them,
Seeking shelter, hoping to enter into that splendour,
But no person was allowed to go in them.
No hearts, no humans: just vanity and vesture.

The dragon moved fearlessly across the ground,
Licking the wounds of the old
And then chewing hard whatever he found.
The whole town gave off an air of blood and cold.

We few ran and reached the city's end
Between sky and land, there was a wide path of moon rays.
Men in white walked peacefully on this band.
I followed, as walking that path seemed to be my sole salvation
from the city's craze.

Eastern Woman

I am a woman, a reason for the world's
Colours, tenderness, and love.
Mistakenly taken as a frail being,
In reality I am brave in the face of every shove.

Strength is the strength that lies inside.
Millions of tempests push me over
Every time I stand up again with pride.
Then I live normally and move on further.

I see only my brothers, travelling along the enlightened paths.
I see only my brothers, not myself, giggling and resting.
How does it feel? It causes pain somewhere in my depths.
Yet I stand up and face all smilingly.

They say I do not belong in this home,
That I am like a bird that perches for a while, only later to fly.
Thus, I am stranger, homeless in my home.
Yet I pick myself up. I do not cry.

Once I flew to rest on a different tree.
Oh, gosh, the offshoot I perched on was frail and ghastly.
I had to kill myself to enable others' glee,
Yet I came through all of this bravely.

The older birds in this tree again
Remind me of my place, and treat me as an outsider.
I feel like a stranger, homeless once again,
But then I repair my broken parts and go further.

With a broken heart and an upset mind,
One's being soon becomes a shrine.
A woman is strong, I think, and then I stand up and find
The strength and patience within myself to walk the line.

For my whole life, homeless and nameless.
Still, I happily raise my kids,
Give them my blood and sweat regardless
Of how they leave me alone when I need their hands.

I come through the ordeal that is the greatest,
The one which brings fruits to this world. How
I sacrifice and subdue my heart for the others in my nest.
How with love and care I watch them grow.

Real power is the power that comes from within.
It enables me to fight the despair, the inequality
The pain, the suffering, and the deprivation.
As woman is resilient, I stand up to all strongly.

Statue

Yes, I just learned the art of sculpting.
This is my first and last work of art. I am trying
To make it an immortal sculpture,
Using soil steeped in tears for a piece that is pictorial,
picturesque.

I am materialising his impressive gestures
And beautiful smile, which is stored in my memories.
The sculpture shares his charming face and broad bosom.
A lifelike statue that has everything going for it but him.

I am incising the beautiful smile he once had on his face.
I wish again to catch a glimpse of it. Or any trace.
But as it will be carved into my statue,
I may enjoy this stand-in for his nearness when I am blue.

His decision to quit smashed my heart.
Inside of me, a big and terrible gap was built.
He did not, but I had wanted him to, come back.
Now, in the form of this statue, I feel his comeback.

This statue is imbued with feelings and has about it the air
Of those days when we would walk on air.
His odour seeps out of the statue's every inch and corner.
I can escape back to those days with him once more.

I remember his piercing, steely, last day's
Glance—and also his indignation, for some unknown reasons
I wish together we could clear the smog and talk.
But now I feel lucky: I'm making his statue, so I feel that he is
back.

The Sea

Wide, wide, shoreless blue water
Left me bemused and petrified.
So pure, the scene is so refreshing.
I'm stunned by the beauty of this bluish water.
The Lord made this world so pretty and dignified.
Somewhere in its depths, a deep secret it seems to be holding.

On the water's surface, the sun's rays are widespread,
Making it amazingly shimmering and sparkling,
As if thousands of pure pearls have come up
From the depths and are now waiting, floating hand in hand,
To be chosen and picked up for being
Parts of some beautiful ornament.

The water has been coloured by varying shades of blue.
The dark, moving clouds are making mischief
By blotting out and then unveiling the sun continuously.
I saw daylight and night appear together, as if one had
jumped ahead in the queue.
When the sun breaks through, after the spell of darkness, for a
brief
It bestows upon the water's surface every shade of blue.

Drama begins with rain pelting down
Out of the blue, followed by big, strong hailstones.
On the surface of the water, as it is hit by the hail,
Millions of dancing little bowls appear and then drown,
Instigating an enchanting music, which mixes
With the waves' sound and makes a marvellous spectacle.

*   *   *

I closed my eyes in enchantment.
Cold breeze touched my face, and my
Thinking froze up, but that of my inner eye.
When the sun broke through the clouds in the sky,
I saw milky rays, in the form of circle, create
A white and dreamy path along which angels or fairies may fly.

A chariot rode down this path of milky rays.
In it, some beautiful people and fairies were seated,
Along with angels and heavenly birds flying around.
All were smiling. How contented they did sound!
They looked to be coming from heaven, those noble souls,
As the good and virtuous are always rewarded.

At the brink of the briny, the procession stopped.
They all scattered, walking up the mountainsides
Fully covered in velvety green grass.
Deep yellow flowers looked to be made of shiny brass.
Hundreds of diamonds rolled down, ready to be picked
Through the sunbeams: a reward, or one of God's blessings.

Over the valley dark clouds loitered
Projecting over the mountains the scene of night and day
Keeping pace with one another, which made the place
A perfect dream and left me in sweet trance.
It brings me alive when I call these scenes to mind.
I hope I'll be virtuous enough to again see this day.

A Wander in the Woods

I awoke and went out with no coat.
I walked and walked and walked, and
Saw in the windy woods a woman who sat.
Her slow whisper was widespread,
her words were weird and unclear.
I wondered what those were?.

Among wild weeds, outside in cold weather,
Wearing her warm, wavy skirt and blue blouse,
I saw her sitting in a wobbly, wooden white chair.
She was wrapping her waistcoat and wellingtons.
The whole spot was filled with a weird, vile smell.
I wondered, *What is it that is whole?*

I waded nearer. I watched and gazed.
My foot crashed into her wellingtons,
From black to white her wellingtons changed.
Oh, she was a witch in the woods.
I was in hot water. O, my day!
Withdraw, withdraw, but where is the way?

That wicked, wizened old woman as
Woe waved her wand and whacked
My waist. At once I went down on muddy weeds

As if struck by a heavy piece of wood. My waist was wrecked.
She placed her wand on my waist. I wavered on weeds.
Wagging her whip, as if in a vortex, she kept me on wind and
weeds.

I wept and wailed and cried and yelled.
That wayward witch smiled wilfully
Wagged her whip as I wallowed in weeds and mud.
I was a weapon for her act of witchery.
She weighed me down with her magic wand
And went about her witchcraft in the way in which she wished.

On my left, she whispered weird words, then
Lowered her wand and wrote on a white chair.
I watched and rushed west in no time, then
Waded through mud and weeds, moving like a bullet after fire
Wild shrieks, whirling whispers, and whacking
Whips were after me, which sped up my running.

Wan, weltering in mud, pale, and wounded,
I went down into whirling water after I slipped.
The deep vortex, when I woke up and opened
My eyelids, was in the woods, was a clock on the room's wall,
clicked
8.00 a.m. Oh, I was wet with sweat.
I watched and went out in the cold wearing my coat.

Under the Sunshine

The day was hot and sunny.
Everybody was looking for
Something cool and shadowy.
All became hectic, red, and brighter.
To be under that sun seemed funny.

Two stepped out of the faculty.
Both were tired; one had a wide yawn.
Feeling too hot, they tried to find anyplace shadowy.
Their comrade appeared from the lawn.
When they saw him, they smiled naïvely.

He joined in, and the three became immersed in laughing,
Sharing the best of their glee,
Regardless of any heat or scorching.
Those three were Ammy, Rehan, and me.
The sun was surprised to see how we were bearing.

It was amazing to see those bold hearts
Standing on that burning spot.
The sun was constantly throwing its hottest beams,
But it failed to make us feel even a bit hot.
We defeated its hottest rays.

Every hotness is bearable
If people can feel the coolness
Of the love, while
They share. A thousand shadows
Cannot make that bliss double.

For 5 July

You, as a couple, are evergreen.
A love like yours is rarely seen.

May God permit you both to live very long.
May God give you everything you need to thrive, as together
you belong.

We hope that you will live happily together,
That there is great harmony between you forever.

Special days are not to miss.
On this one, we hope for your bliss.

Your children wish you all the best, and we pray
On 5 July, which is an auspicious day.

It's Me

I'd rather avoid exposing myself,
But if I'm asked to, I refuse not.
I always eat cherries to please myself
But if you give me plum, I'll like it not.

Mother asks me to study hard,
But I pay heed not.
I like to watch movie and listen to bard
I open my books, but they attract me not.

I never follow a fad.
What people say, I care not.
I often argue with my dad,
But in the case of mother I dare not.

I write poetry, and I widely yawn at
The rules for doing so, which I follow not.
My poetry follows the rules I create.
I warn every reader to forget me not.

Deep Shadows

We were sitting in white moonlight
Holding each other in our eyes,
Lost both in the scene and in deep delight.
Fair, milky moonlight gave rise
To hot air. While a cold breeze was blowing
Across our locks, leaves were whispering,
That very near, the flowers were being.

The river flowing nearby was creating
The light music of the night.
All waves mingled and were pushing
Each other into a row to set a sight,
Pervading the whole by a pleasant noise.
Swiftly passing, some impatient waves
Rubbed and heated the fusing stones.

We soaked in night's glitter so deeply
And were enraptured by the rejoicing radiance,
Amazed and stunned by the beauty
Of widespread moonlight and by its magnificence.
Bemused as the peacock danced.
The lure of the scene shed
Its mellow feelings on a mild grass bed.

Pearls of dew on the weeds added to the sublime
Sight. Our hearts were throbbing.
Our moods were moulding. And I deem
Nature to be so pleasingly fomenting,
Such as, a light drizzle begins and a cold breeze blows,
A peacock dances and a pipit's voice soothes.
Then our locks were blown, and we came close.

Fear

No one is with me here.
I am going alone.
Before me, my fate lies bare.
Everything seems to be gone.

I am alone, alone, and there is no one to care.

My doings took me where?
All have turned their hearts.
I am left with nothing. Do I dare
Say that soon will be used up my stores?

I am alone and no one cares.

Their doing anything for me is harder.
Am I to be taken as an unfortunate?
From me people are very, very far.
O God, why have you left gloominess in my fate?

I am feeling alone and that no one is to care.

Stepping ahead, the path is deeply sheer.
I am afraid of the dark and of the unknown.
The pain of loneliness is something my mind has to bear.
My wings and colours all are blown.

I am going alone. No one is here.

Flood of Rain

Rainwater submerged a beautiful town
With water running from house to house.
Fields, flowers, and birds, all were down
Alleys, valleys, and wells, altogether soaked.
Smell of death was travelling everywhere through town.

A mother of four was very optimistic, very hopeful.
Water had poured inside her small house.
Life for her was never restful.
Every wrinkle had a story, but she knew that
Even a barren stone, if tries, can make life joyful.

She thought to lead the children towards the light of hope.
Hardships shouldn't dry and rust their innocent hearts.
They must learn to endure when their hope and happiness drop
This was but one of life's low points, with which
They must learn to cope.

A kid uttered that his school uniform was wetting.
"So sad, it is dripping heavily all along the way.
Piercingly cold and very scary the night is getting.
How can I sleep, how can I dream?
When will come the light of morning?"

Mum said that God had chosen them to walk this friction-filled
path.
"The Lord trusts your courage, power, and glory.
All sorrows, hardships, and afflictions give you strength,
Shape your thoughts, and test your patience.
Only then you can achieve right growth."

"Go on, dream, always dream.
The dark night is a short break from life.
Soon, the bright light of dawn will welcome
You, and you'll pass your days with a smile,
But only if you first learn to cope with your sorrows and gloom.

"All of these drops which are separately dripping
Will come together and make a
Shiny chariot for you. You will find yourself flying
High, and ever higher, as you learn to soar through pain.
You'll never come down, as these drops will strengthen your
wing."

Then she collected and together joined
Some floating, broken parts of house stuff.
Trying to save the remaining three kids' lives, energetically she
moved.
She saw some huge men wearing clothes that shone,
And the road heading towards city, which they showed.

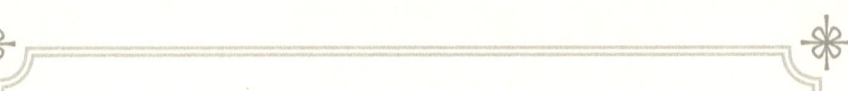

Hours and hours in water, the mother dragged the board.
When cold water swallowed one more kid, after a while,
Still she saw the huge people dressed
In shining clothes, instructing her to move in the right way.
She did not fail. Through the difficulty she dared.

Frozen with cold, one more kid flumped down into the water.
But at last, with only one child left, she reached in to see the glimmer.

www.ingramcontent.com/pod-product-compliance
Lightning Source LLC
Chambersburg PA
CBHW021026180526
45163CB00005B/2134